CONTENTS

INTRODUCTION

*I*n hopes of curbing harsh disciplinary policies and high suspension rates in Massachusetts' schools, the Massachusetts legislature enacted Chapter 222[1] in 2014. Among other reforms, Chapter 222 calls for schools to modify codes of conduct to apply suspensions only as a last resort for non-drug, non-violent, non-criminal related infractions.[2] Chapter 222 does not apply to students charged with a felony offense (such as possession of narcotics or weapons) under section 37H½ of Chapter 71.[3] Thus, this small book does not address suspensions or expulsions for felony offenses; it only discusses out-of-school suspensions for Category 18 offenses.[4]

Even with the enactment of Chapter 222, Massachusetts' charter schools still disciplined students with exclusionary pun-

---

[1] 2012 Mass. Ch. 222.

[2] Since this is category 18 on the discipline data collected and reported by the Massachusetts Department of Education, I will refer to non-drug, non-violent, non-criminal related offenses as Category 18 offenses.

[3] *Mass. Gen. Laws* ch. 71 § 37H½ (2014).

[4] This category should be broken down further in order to allow for accurate assessments of the reasons for student suspensions. For instance, the category should include for how long students were suspended and for what specific offenses.

ishments[5] for minor offenses more often than public schools during the 2014-2015 school year.[6] Even more troubling, Boston charter schools suspended low-income students, students with disabilities, and students of color at higher rates than they did white students.[7] Through an analysis of two Boston charter schools' codes of conduct[8] and data on out-of-school suspensions at six Massachusetts charter schools,[9] this book shows that charter schools' exclusionary disciplinary practices disproportionately affect Black and Latino students (especially males).[10]

Studies show that students who were suspended are more likely to drop out of school, engage in criminal activity, and encounter the criminal justice system.[11] Thus, exclusionary disciplinary methods used by some Boston charter schools have a disparate impact on poor youth of color—thereby reducing their chances of academic and future professional success and productive citizenship. Such adverse impact clearly violates the philosophical and ethical vision espoused in *Brown*

---

[5] "Exclusionary punishments" include any disciplinary measures that exclude students from participating in daily classroom life, but particularly in-school and out-of-school suspensions and expulsions.

[6] This is the latest data available. *See* http://profiles.doe.mass.edu/state_report/ssdr.aspx (accessed June 10, 2015).

[7] James Vaznis, *Charter Schools Suspend More than Traditional Schools*, BOSTON GLOBE (Nov. 19, 2014), https://www.bostonglobe.com/metro/2014/11/19/report-cites-high-suspension-rates-for-charter-schools/AF3y7UxpQJsGtytOP7I6RJ/story.html

[8] The two schools chosen were the ones with the two highest out-of-school suspension rates for Category 18 offenses during the 2014-2015 school year. The schools are Roxbury Preparatory Charter (38.6%) and City on a Hill Charter School, Dudley Square Campus (33%).

[9] Massachusetts is the state of focus because Chapter 222 requires that schools report disciplinary data each school year. This comprehensive database facilitates research.

[10] *See* Kerrin Wolf et al., *Charting School Discipline*, 48 URB. LAW. 1 (2016) (surveying current charter school exclusionary disciplinary practices and their effects on students of color).

[11] Cherry Henault, *Chalk Talk: Zero Tolerance in Schools*, 30 J.L. & EDUC. 547 (2001).

v. Board of Education.[12] But I argue the solution is not found in the judicial system, as legal precedent shows the judiciary deferring to schools and the legislature to handle the "political" question of student discipline and rights.[13]

In view of the many unsuccessful attempts to litigate disparate impact and due process claims by students and their advocates against public and charter schools,[14] this book asserts that school cultures themselves need to change and that legislatures should seek to curb arbitrary and capricious[15] suspensions by administrators, especially of already vulnerable populations like poor Black and Latino students. In other words, school officials need to work together with the surrounding community to meet the unique needs of impoverished students of color, perhaps by recruiting more school officials and teachers from within those communities.[16] And legislatures should go

---

[12] *Brown v. Bd. of Educ.*, 347 U.S. 483, 493 (1954) ("Today, education is perhaps the most important function of state and local governments. Compulsory school attendance laws and the great expenditures for education both demonstrate our recognition of the importance of education to our democratic society. It is required in the performance of our most basic public responsibilities, even service in the armed forces. It is the very foundation of good citizenship. Today it is a principal instrument in awakening the child to cultural values, in preparing him for later professional training, and in helping him to adjust normally to his environment. In these days, it is doubtful that any child may reasonably be expected to succeed in life if he is denied the opportunity of an education. Such an opportunity, where the state has undertaken to provide it, is a right which must be made available to all on equal terms.").

[13] *See* DERRICK BELL, SILENT COVENANTS: BROWN V. BOARD OF EDUCATION AND THE UNFULFILLED HOPES FOR RACIAL REFORM 200 (2004) (suggesting the need for people of color and other marginalized communities to seek justice by "relying less on the courts to advance racial justice goals" and more on community efforts).

[14] *Id; See also* Melanie R. Jarboe, Note, *"Expelled to Nowhere": School Exclusion Laws in Massachusetts*, 31 B.C. THIRD WORLD L.J. 343 (2011) (noting that judicial challenges to charter schools by claimants arguing discrimination, disparate impact, and violation of due process have been largely unsuccessful because most courts see the issue as a political one best suited for the legislature).

[15] *Doe v. Superintendent of Schs. of Stoughton*, 437 Mass. 1, 5 (2002) (Massachusetts courts "will overturn a superintendent's decision to suspend a student only it is arbitrary and capricious, so as to constitute an abuse of discretion.").

[16] BELL, *supra* note 13.

beyond Chapter 222 to also provide financial incentives to schools that phase out exclusionary and punitive disciplinary methods and instead institute restorative and other justice-based disciplinary methods.[17]

A caveat is in order: this book does not advocate eradicating exclusionary disciplinary polices for students caught with deadly weapons on campus, or for students grossly bullying and/or threatening other students or faculty.[18] Yet, statistics show that charter and public schools experience very minimal felony offenses, so the issue is not the application of exclusionary disciplinary methods for major felony offenses, but rather the capricious application of such disciplinary methods for minor or Category 18 offenses.[19] As noted above, this book also does not suggest that courts are in a superior position vis-à-vis teachers in determining best disciplinary practices for their schools.[20] Determining school policy, however, should be a joint venture among all community stakeholders, including parents, teachers, administrators, the students themselves, and even local business and political leaders.[21] After all, as the African proverb says, it takes a village to raise a child.

Part I discusses the current state of charter schools in Massachusetts, along with an examination of the disciplinary

---

[17] Marilyn Armour, *Restorative Practices: Righting the Wrongs of Exclusionary School Discipline*, 50 U. RICH. L. REV. 999 (2016).

[18] Christina L. Anderson, Comment, *Double Jeopardy: The Modern Dilemma for Juvenile Justice*, 152 U. PA. L. REV. 1181 (2004) (calling for a combination of restorative and punitive techniques in a school).

[19] *Id.*

[20] *See Doe v. Superintendent of Schs. of Stoughton*, 437 Mass. 1, 13 (2002) ("Because school officials are in the best position to determine when a student's actions threaten the safety and welfare of other students, we must grant school officials substantial deference in their disciplinary choices.").

[21] Armour, *supra* note 17.

methods employed by two charter schools that suspend at higher percentages than the other schools. Part I also highlights suspension data at six Boston charter schools and district wide and delves into the consequences of such suspensions for poor Black and Latino males, with particular attention to the school-to-prison pipeline.

Part II traces the arduous—and often unsuccessful—trajectory of legal challenges to exclusionary disciplinary practices and other anti-student rights policies in an effort to underscore the need for less judicial solutions, and more local and legislative solutions. It does this by analyzing five landmark cases in the struggle for student rights: three Supreme Court decisions, one Massachusetts Supreme Judicial Court decision, and one Massachusetts trail-court decision.

Through an analysis of Chapter 222, Part III proposes that strategic solutions to the disproportionate application of exclusionary disciplinary policies and practices are best developed by pressuring school communities themselves to rethink disciplinary codes of conduct and their application. Citizens should also pressure the legislative branch at the federal, state, and local levels to invest in more progressive disciplinary policies that value dealing with minor, Category 18 offenses in restorative ways that ultimately keep students in the classroom. Grassroots organizations and vigilant citizens also offer the best line of defense against unacceptable educational policies. Such organizations also ensure the local application of legislative reforms and policies.

PART I
Setting the Stage: Exclusionary Discipline at Charter Schools, and Its Consequences

When they voted November 2016, the citizens of Massachusetts struck down Question 2, which would have paved the way for the creation of twelve charter schools per year, with preference given to charter proposals in the lowest-performing districts. Of course, these districts contain the Commonwealth's poorest students, the vast majority of whom are students of color. And charter schools in Massachusetts already contain mostly Black and Latino students.[22] Had voters approved Question 2 in November, the measure would have allowed an increase to the eighty-one charter schools already in the Commonwealth.

The ballot measure seems to have equal support and opposition. What seems to trouble liberal politicians and mostly white liberal activists is that Black and Latino parents seem to "feel more comfortable in academically rigorous, heavily minority schools than in schools with whiter student bodies."[23]

---

[22] *See* ERICA FRANKENBERG, THE CIVIL RIGHTS PROJECT 81 (2010) (noting the prevalence in the North of "apartheid charter schools," that is, schools with majority Black and/or Latino students).

[23] Davis Scharfenberg, *Racial Aspects Tinge Mass. Charter Debate*, BOSTON GLOBE (Mar. 28, 2016), https://www.bostonglobe.com/metro/2016/03/27/charter-school-fight-racial-complication/Wc4U2OwnIzKFPrGakDBYjL/story.html.

But opponents say these sentiments are the result of misinformation and false expectations of what charter schools actually do. After speaking with some parents in the town of Dorchester during my studies at the Harvard Graduate School of Education, I discovered that parents indeed have a very limited understanding of what a charter school even is or does.

Rise of Charter Schools

Roxbury Preparatory Charter School offers the following definition:

> A charter school is an independently run public school granted greater flexibility in its operations, in return for greater accountability for performance. The 'charter' establishing each school is a performance contract detailing the school's mission, program, students served, performance goals, and methods of assessments.[24]

Charters receive public funding and are supposed to be open to all students living in the district.[25] Yet, because of high demand some charter schools run a lottery that often excludes students of color with disabilities from gaining admission— leaving these vulnerable students with less choices of schools.[26] Charter schools are private as well because "they are operated by private boards of directors under a charter agreement with

---

[24] *Frequently Asked Questions About Public, Charter Schools*, UNCOMMON SCHOOLS, http://www.uncommonschools.org/faq-what-is-charter-school (last visited Jun. 24, 2016). Uncommon Schools is the charter management organization that runs several charter schools, including Roxbury Preparatory.

[25] Wolf et al., *supra* note 10.

[26] DAVID WHITMAN, SWEATING THE SMALL STUFF: INNER-CITY SCHOOLS AND THE NEW PATERNALISM (2008).

the charter authorizer."[27] Forty-two states currently house charter schools, which now seem like a fixture in the current U.S. educational landscape—especially with the recent appointment of Nancy Devos as President Trump's Secretary of Education.[28]

The Bush Administration's No Child Left Behind Act ("NCLB") and the Obama Administration's Race to the Top Initiative ("Race Initiative") accelerated the growth of charter schools.[29] NCLB "incorporates market-based reforms" that require schools to meet certain yearly academic benchmarks for all students.[30] Students' performance on standardized tests serves as the measuring stick for academic success.[31] A school that fails to meet the federally mandated benchmark for two consecutive years must allow students to transfer to other schools, and schools that fail to meet the benchmark for five consecutive years must relinquish control to the state.[32] The state may then close the school and grant a charter to a private board of directors, who in turn opens a charter school where the "failing" public school once stood.[33] The charter school

---

[27] Wolf et al., *supra* note 10, at 4.

[28] Scharfenberg, *supra* note 23.

[29] Erika K. Wilson, *Gentrification and Urban Public School Reforms: The Interest Divergence Dilemma*, 118 W. VA. L. REV. 677 (2015).

[30] *Id.* at 703.

[31] Though it is beyond the scope of this paper, scholars note that both NCLB and the Race Initiative have "ushered in high stakes testing—transforming schools into production factories. Students who acted up are removed so that teachers can focus on the remaining students, thereby separating out those who will succeed from those who will fail." Thus, some scholars make the connection between charter schools' fixation on test scores and their high suspension rates of students of colors with disabilities. Armour, *supra* note, at 1001.

[32] Wilson, *supra* note 29.

[33] *Id.*

then has flexibility in determining its academic and disciplinary policies.

The Race Initiative, spearheaded by former Secretary of Education Arne Duncan, provides competitive grant funding to states that "ensure successful conditions for high-performing charters and other innovative schools."[34] Thus, the Race Initiative explicitly encourages the creation of charter schools. Indeed, to compete for the grant funding, many states have facilitated the process for boards of directors to acquire charters.[35] Undergirding these market-based reforms is the theory that by expanding charter schools, students will have more choices of where to attend school.[36] Further, charter school proponents argue that charter schools will incentivize public schools to close the achievement gap or else face their own demise.

The charter school reform movement has thrived due to the "closing [of] so-called under-enrolled or poor performing traditional schools and increasing the number of charter schools in urban areas."[37] Contrary to the optimism of parents in Massachusetts, research shows that "the majority of poor and minority students are more likely to enroll in charter schools that perform equivalent to or worse than traditional public schools."[38] And of concern here, these poor students of

---

[34] U.S. Dep't of Educ., Race to the Top Program Executive Summary 1 (2009), http://www2.ed.gov/programs/racetothetop/executive-summary.pdf (last accessed Jun. 28, 2016).

[35] Wilson, *supra* note 29.

[36] Conservatives tend to argue that charter schools reflect neo-liberal free-market ideologies of unregulated choice. *But see* Whitman, *supra* note 26, at 286 ("Yet [charter schools] are hardly free-market icons. They exert a supervisory authority over student lives that would make libertarians squirm if adults rather than teens sat in students' seats.").

[37] Wilson, *supra* note 29, at 702-703.

[38] *Id.* at 713.

color enroll in charter schools that disproportionately discipline them for minor offenses—thus affecting their chances of academic, civic, personal, and professional success.

Zero-Tolerance and Exclusionary Discipline Practices, the Discipline Gap, and Sweating the Small Stuff

According to the anti-charter school group Quality Education for Every Student (QUEST), one of the issues plaguing the existing eighty-one charter schools in Massachusetts is the disparate rates of suspensions of Black and Latino students compared to their white counterparts.[39] A cursory look at the most recent data shows that Massachusetts charter schools did indeed suspend Black and Latino students at higher rates than did the Commonwealth's public schools. In fact, on the list of schools that disciplined students most with out-of-school suspensions for Category 18 offenses, the top twenty-one are all charter schools, with ranges from 38.6% to 6.4%. Southbridge Middle/High School is the first traditional public school to appear on the list, at twenty-two, with a 5.8% out-of-school suspension rate for Category 18 offenses. Curiously, Southbridge by far had the largest student population of the schools in the top twenty-two, with 2,437 students. Yet Southbridge suspended students at a far less rate than the smaller Roxbury Prep (with 909 total students) and the significantly smaller City on a Hill Charter School (with 197 total students). Raw numbers speak for themselves: Roxbury Prep and City on a Hill together disciplined 420 students for Category 18 offenses, while Southbridge disciplined only 193 students for similar of-

---

[39] Scharfenberg, *supra* note 23.

fenses. What accounts for this disparity among Charter schools and traditional public schools?

Charter schools have wide latitude to develop their disciplinary policies.[40] Though charter schools are bound by state regulations (such as 37H), they have wide discretion in developing and enforcing disciplinary measures—thus setting the tone for school culture.[41] The high rates of out-of-school suspensions and discipline of students suggest that charter schools rely on a stricter, harsher disciplinary scheme compared to traditional public schools.[42] According to a recent study of Philadelphia charter schools codes of conducts, these schools "turn too quickly to exclusionary school discipline as a response to student misbehavior."[43] The study also showed that administrators at these schools had almost unfettered discretion in deciding what offenses merited suspensions.[44]

While the data reflect the growing suspensions of charter school students, little research exists on "the role of charter school disciplinary practices and their potential effects on charter school students."[45] The existing data, however, should cause concern to parents, students, educators, legislatures, and the wider community.[46] Further, the charter school movement is gaining steam, especially in Massachusetts, so research on the effects of charter school disciplinary polices is crucial to accu-

---

[40] Wolf et al., *supra* note 10, at 6.

[41] *Id.* at 11.

[42] Whitman, *supra* note 26, at 37 ("[T]he most distinctive feature of … paternalistic charter schools is that they are fixated on curbing disorder.").

[43] Wolf et al., *supra* note 10, at 36.

[44] *Id.*

[45] *Id.* at 1.

[46] *Id.*

rately assess the pros and cons of current exclusionary practices on all students, but particularly on Black and Latino students.[47] Recent empirical and qualitative research is also indispensible for legislatures to gauge adherence to Chapter 222's requirement that school officials refrain from using out-of-school suspensions for Category 18 offenses until they exhaust all other alternatives.

Charter schools like Roxbury Prep and City on a Hill, however, seemingly suspend students at will for minor offenses. Their polices reflect a zero-tolerance approach.[48] Zero-tolerance refers to disciplinary policies that severely punish all offenses, regardless of the severity of the crime and with no consideration of the student's background or the context.[49] During an interview for the Dean of Discipline position at a Boston charter school known for its strict disciplinary polices and which predominately served Black and Latino students, I was asked to rank hypothetical offenses in severity from 1-10. I chose as the physical bullying of a student by a fellow student as the most severe, and the chewing of gum by a student during class as the least severe. The Vice Principal admonished my choices, stating that at their charter school, faculty and staff viewed all offenses as equally adverse to the school's culture of discipline.

This anecdote echoes the assertion that most out-of-school suspensions at charter schools "are dispensed for minor

---

[47] *Id.*

[48] The first book to popularize the concept of no-excuses, zero-tolerance schools was SAMUEL CASEY CARTER, NO EXCUSES: LESSONS FROM 21 HIGH-PERFORMING, HIGH-POVERTY SCHOOLS (2001).

[49] Henault, *supra* note 11.

noncompliance or disrespect…."[50] Indeed, at Roxbury Prep, only four students were disciplined for having a "weapon on school premises," one for "bullying," five for "non-sexual physical assault," twenty-two for "physical fights," and six for possession of "illegal substances." Yet, while no students were suspended or expelled for these more serious infractions, 38.6% students were suspended out-of-school for Category 18 offenses. Some of these "offenses" might even have been down right silly, such as rolling of the eyes or chewing gum in class.[51]

Early childhood and adolescence are vital periods for the healthy development of any person.[52] Educators have traditionally viewed minor student misconduct as integral to healthy child and adolescent development. Consequently, educators have traditionally responded to minor misconduct with school-based interventions that allow the student to reflect and learn from the behavior.[53] But "current punitive and exclusionary practices are predicated on the belief that school-based misbehavior is evidence of a dangerous and growing trend of out-of-control youth."[54] Some educators and community members see Black and Latino youth as more dangerous and out-of-control than white or Asian youth. These adults cite youth of color's adherence to hip-hop culture, their socioeconomic back-

---

[50] Anderson, *supra* note 18, at 1192.

[51] BELL HOOKS, TEACHING TO TRANSGRESS: EDUCATION AS THE PRACTICE OF FREEDOM 178 (1994) ("[L]oudness, anger, emotional outbursts, and even something as seemingly innocent as unrestrained laughter were deemed unacceptable vulgar disruptions of classroom social order.").

[52] *See* Joan Goodman, *Charter Management Organizations and the Regulated Environment: Is It Worth the Price?*, 42 EDUC. RES. 89 (2013).

[53] *See* Armour, *supra* note 17.

[54] *Id.* at 1000.

grounds, their broken families, and their impoverished, crime-ridden neighborhoods.[55] It is no surprise that Black students, particularly Black males, are expelled and suspended at higher rates than white students nationwide—and at Massachusetts charter schools.[56]

Indeed, educational and legal scholars and activists have criticized zero-tolerance policies and its progeny as unfair and arbitrary, particularly when applied to poor students of color.[57] While schools created the policies to establish and ensure safe schools, the available research shows the policies "are increasingly ineffective, generating racial disproportionality in discipline, academic failure, high dropout rates, and a clear school-to-prison pipeline."[58] All twenty-one top suspending charter schools in Massachusetts suspended Black and Latino students at higher (sometimes double) rates than they did whites and Asians for Category 18 offenses. The only exception is the mostly all-white Amesbury Academy Charter School, whose forty-five out of fifty-one students were white. Amesbury had no Black students and only two Latino students, so it makes sense they would suspend whites at a higher ratio.

Again, the statistics speak for themselves. I chose to compare six out of the twenty-one charter schools to underscore the disparity of out-of-school suspensions for Category 18 offenses among four racial groups: Blacks, Latinos, whites,

---

[55] *See* PRUDENCE CARTER, KEEPIN' IT REAL: SCHOOL SUCCESS BEYOND BLACK AND WHITE (2007).

[56] Melanie R. Jarboe, Note, *"Expelled to Nowhere": School Exclusion Laws in Massachusetts*, 31 B.C. THIRD WORLD L.J. 343 (2011).

[57] Henault, *supra* note 11, at 547 ("[P]erhaps the most disturbing aspect of [zero-tolerance policies] is its apparent disparate impact on minority students.").

[58] Armour, *supra* note 17, at 999.

and Asians.[59] The data reveal that Black and Latino students served out-of-school suspensions at higher rates than did white and Asian students. Skeptics might claim that higher suspension rates among students of color is inevitable due to the fact that the majority of charter schools enroll a majority Black and Latino population. But at Hampden Charter School, the majority of students were white (162) and yet they were suspended only 4.9% of the time. There were only seventy-six Black students, with 11.8% suspended. Similarly, at City on a Hill Charter in New Bedford, Black students were suspended at higher rates than whites, even though Black students numbered less than whites in the general student population. The same was true at Excel Academy.

Overall, the numbers show that Black students received out-of-school suspensions more frequently than White and even Latino students for Category 18 offenses. The data seem to bolster the claim that "black makes receive more frequent and harsh discipline than any other minority group" and noticeably more so than whites.[60] Notably, Asian students were not suspended or disciplined at all at any of the twenty-one charter schools—which raises the possibility that educators perceive them as the model minority.[61] On the other side of the spectrum, educators may perceive Black and Latino youth as deviant minority groups in need of immediate and harsh discipline for even the most minor infractions. Attorneys at the

---

[59] Refer to page 53, Appendix I, for data chart.

[60] Henault, *supra* note 11, at 551.

[61] *See* VIVIAN S. LOUIE, COMPELLED TO EXCEL: IMMIGRATION, EDUCATION, AND OPPORTUNITIES AMONG CHINESE AMERICANS (2004).

Harvard Civil Rights Project on Zero Tolerance noted almost sixteen years ago that racial profiling informed the decisions of educators to discipline Black and Latino youth.[62] Racial bias, they claimed, played an integral role in student discipline—with Black and Latino students more likely to be disciplined for subjective and minor offenses like "defiance of authority" and "disrespect for authority."[63]

Harmful Effects on School Culture and on Students

Zero-tolerance and exclusionary disciplinary polices negatively affect school culture and the students themselves, particularly Black and Latino males.[64] Studies suggest that schools with harsh disciplinary policies create and sustain strained relationships between students and faculty, students and administrators, and even among students themselves.[65] Black and Latino males perceive the arbitrary application of harsh disciplinary practices as an affront to their dignity as members of particular racial groups.[66] Further, when adults show little regard for a particular student's personal history, the context within which the offense was committed, and the student's own motivations for committing the offense, teachers

---

[62] Henault, *supra* note 11.

[63] *Id.* at 551.

[64] Scholar Angela Valenzuela argues that students act like they do not care about school to protest their powerlessness before institutions that constantly judge and categorize them in an attempt to eventually normalize them. Students, in other words, engage in acts of resistance to institutions they perceive are trying to supplant their own cultures. ANGELA VALENZUELA, SUBTRACTIVE SCHOOLING: U.S.-MEXICAN YOUTH AND THE POLITICS OF CARING 61 (1999).

[65] Wolf et al., *supra* note 10, at 14 (highlighting the fierce competition among students to stand out as model citizens in order to reap rewards, such as casual dress days. These rewards serve to differentiate "model" students and "deviant" students, which in turn creates animosity and even jealousy among students).

[66] Henault, *supra* note 11.

and administrators may send the message to students that they do not perceive them as human beings deserving of attention and respect.[67] Disregard for personal history and context dehumanizes the student, allowing administrators to punish that student without considering the punitive effects on the student, school culture, or wider community.[68] When Black and Latino males receive harsher punishments than whites for committing similar minor offenses, these Black and Latino males may form a skewed perception of justice and develop a negative attitude toward authority or law enforcement figures.[69] These factors create at best a tense and at worst a volatile environment wherein untrusting and seemingly uncaring relationships are the norm.[70]

Schools provide suspended students very little incentives to reflect and learn from their behaviors and mistakes.[71] Instead, students perceive suspensions, especially suspensions for minor infractions, as a school's easy way out to not deal with students the school considers "troublesome."[72] And, as discussed, educators seem to perceive Black and Latino males, particularly those who come from impoverished homes, as more "troublesome" than any other student group.[73] Thus, Black and Latino students may internalize suspensions as proof that the world is against them, which in turn might lead them

---

[67] *Id.*

[68] Jarboe, *supra* note 56.

[69] Henault, *supra* note 11.

[70] *Id.*

[71] Jarboe, *supra* note 56.

[72] *Id.*

[73] Armour, *supra* note 17.

to ask why they should attempt to fit in?[74] One writer even suggests that disparate application of harsh exclusionary discipline breeds "deviant" behavior in groups already at risk for such behavior.[75]

Apart from fostering a countercultural, anti-establishment attitude, exclusionary discipline also reifies the already unequal life opportunities afforded poor Black and Latino youth, compared to wealthy, white youth. Sociologist Annette Lareau notes that "inequality permeates" even a child's early years.[76] Some children begin the race of life at mile marker five, while others begin at zero.[77] Lareau argues that upper- and middle-class children in her study developed a "sense of entitlement," while poor and working-class children developed a "sense of constraint" when engaging institutions, such as schools.[78] Within a school setting, children exhibit a "sense of entitlement" when they comfortably assert their individual preferences during class interactions, and when they feel no hesitation in questioning a teacher or other adult regarding any matters they may not agree with.[79] Clearly, upper- and middle-class children develop a sense of comfort and agency in knowing that while they can play within the bounds of the school

---

[74] ANGELA VALENZUELA, SUBTRACTIVE SCHOOLING: U.S.-MEXICAN YOUTH AND THE POLITICS OF CARING 62 (1999) ("Rather than building on students' cultural, linguistic, and community-based knowledge, schools... typically subtract these resources. Psychic and emotional withdrawal from schooling are symptomatic of students' rejection of subtractive schooling and a curriculum they perceive as uninteresting, irrelevant, and test-driven.").

[75] Anderson, *supra* note 18. I do not agree with employing the term "deviant" to refer to children and adolescents.

[76] ANNETTE LAREAU, UNEQUAL CHILDHOOD: CLASS, RACE, AND FAMILY LIFE (2003).

[77] *Id.*

[78] *Id.* at 6.

[79] *Id.*

system, they can also question it when a matter is disagreeable to them.[80]

In contrast, poor and working-class children developed a "sense of constraint" in school settings.[81] Lareau notes that these students (almost of all whom were Black and Latino) neither asserted their preferences at school, nor developed the sense of agency so prevalent among the wealthier, white students.[82] She also underscores that poor and working-class parents were less involved in their children's school life.[83] This might explain why certain parents view the emergence of charter schools as positive: these schools, in their minds, will instill in their children the scholastic, behavioral and cultural mores that parents simply cannot,[84] either because of time constraints or because parents feel incompetent to teach their children dominant cultural repertoires.[85]

Yet, charter schools that employ an exclusionary disciplinary system do not instill in students behavioral and cultural mores that will lead to a successful adult life.[86] On the contrary, such no-excuses, harsh disciplinary systems fail to present students with viable choices that are integral to a child's ethical-decision making development.[87] These schools present students with no meaningful choices other than suspensions or

---

[80] *Id.*

[81] *Id.*

[82] *Id.*

[83] *Id.*

[84] Scharfenberg, *supra* note 23.

[85] LAREAU, *supra* note 76.

[86] WHITMAN, *supra* note 26, at 36 ("Paternalistic schools assume that disadvantaged students do best when structure and expectations are crystal clear, rather than presuming that kids should learn to figure things out for themselves.").

[87] Goodman, *supra* note 52.

expulsions for even minor offenses.[88] Thus, interactional skills take a back seat to blind obedience and compliance with the charter school's prescriptive code of conduct.[89] Chances for student grievances are few, and teachers and administrators instill fear in the consequences of breaking any rule, however minor.[90] This culture of repression and strict obedience prevents Black and Latino students from developing agency, creativity, independence, and assertiveness—all skills fostered among wealthier, white students.[91] The effects of exclusionary discipline, however, go beyond the confines of the school campus; they affect the very communities within which schools are located, as evident from the effects of the school-to-prison pipeline.[92]

School-To-Prison Pipeline

The school-to-prison pipelines refers to the complex process by which school administrators and teachers discipline Black and Latino males more arbitrarily and harshly than they do white students,[93] which then increases the likelihood that Black and Latino males will encounter the criminal justice and penal system.[94] The boom of out-of-school suspensions has a

---

[88] *Id.*

[89] *Id.*

[90] WHITMAN, *supra* note 26.

[91] Goodman, *supra* note 52.

[92] Judith A.M. Scully, *Examining and Dismantling the School-To-Prison Pipeline: Strategies for a Better Future*, 68 ARK. L. REV. 959 (2016).

[93] *Id.* at 960 ("African American students who violate the school rules are more likely to face multi-day suspensions and generally harsher punishment than White students who engage in the same kind of conduct.").

[94] *Id.*

direct correlation to the increase of the prison-industrial complex.[95] Indeed, some refer to the U.S. as the "incarceration nation."[96] The rise in the U.S. prison population is the direct result of the "get tough on crime" stance prominent among politicians and the media in the late 1980s and early 1990s.[97] Federal law enforcement agencies widely implemented zero-tolerance policies during the late 80s and early 90s to wage the "war on drugs."[98]

Juvenile crime rates also rose during this time period,[99] prompting panic among politicians, the media, and educators.[100] Children and teenagers suddenly became Public Enemy #1, with reports constantly underscoring their lawlessness and reckless behaviors.[101] These reports perpetuated the prevailing myth of contemporary teenagers as a generation of superpredators—the worst criminal adolescent generation in U.S. history.[102] But the media did not label all children as superpredators. Magazine articles and news reports featured Black youth (especially Black boys) as the ultimate superpredator.[103] Black youth were portrayed as "an army of thugs" seeking to cause harm to innocent citizens working diligently to pursue the

---

[95] Jarboe, *supra* note 56.

[96] Scully, *supra* note 92, at 963 (noting that the U.S. currently holds the dubious distinction of having the highest incarceration rates in the world).

[97] Henault, *supra* note 11.

[98] *Id.*

[99] Wolf et al., *supra* note 10, at 14.

[100] Jarboe, *supra* note 56.

[101] Jarboe, *supra* note 56.

[102] Anderson, *supra* note 18, at 1181.

[103] Scully, *supra* note 92, at 965 (explaining that the media circulated several stories of Black boys holding handguns and running unconstrained committing several crimes in residential and commercial settings).

"American dream."[104] Politicians and law enforcement therefore felt a need to lock these "monsters" up to preserve law and order; rehabilitation was never an option, even for minor offenses.[105] Thus began the mass demonization, criminalization, and incarceration of children and adolescents, particularly Black and Latino adolescents.[106]

The public school became one of the spaces politicians and law enforcement felt needed strict regulation. Hence, the Federal Government enacted two pieces of legislation in 1994: The Gun Free Schools Act and The Violent Crime Control and Law Enforcement Act.[107] The Gun Free Act called for a zero-tolerance approach to students found with weapons on campus. Schools were supposed to expel any students with weapons, and schools were advised to report the student to law enforcement.[108] Yet schools and school districts began applying a similar zero-tolerance approach to even the most trivial student misbehavior[109]—misbehavior that only some years prior would have been handled with a verbal warning by a teacher, administrator or parent.[110]

Students have been suspended and even arrested for writing "Okay" on a desk or for repeatedly passing gas in a

---

[104] *Id.* at 966 (recounting that the image of the "black male criminal" also emerged during this time, along with the Black female crack head and other derogatory imagery).

[105] *Id.*

[106] Henault, *supra* note 11; Anderson, *supra* note 18.

[107] Wolf et al., *supra* note 10.

[108] *Id.*

[109] *Id.*

[110] Scully, *supra* note 92, at 969 (noting that schools suspended students out-of-school for tardiness, skipping school or class, and for asking too many questions in class. Other incidents reported include public affection, refusing to sit in class, and making noises in class or in the hallways).

classroom.[111] And as the data show, most out-of-school suspensions in Massachusetts charter schools occurred for Category 18 offenses, many of which are trivial incidents. On the one hand, educators perceive Black and Latino youth as "out-of-control" and in need of serious behavior modification, even for trivial misbehavior.[112] On the other hand, educators view trivial misbehavior by white students as "youthful mistakes" that present no threat to authority or the status quo.[113] Just as law enforcement perceived Black youth during the 90s as superpredators, today's charter school educators seem to view Black and Latino youth as especially deviant characters in need of constant surveillance and harsh, tough punishment, even for minor mishaps.[114]

Disparate and arbitrary out-of-school suspensions for trivial misbehavior push students out of the school system and directly into the criminal justice, penal system.[115] Black and Latino males are already at risk for run-ins with law enforcement notwithstanding their academic achievements or failures.[116]

---

[111] *Id.* at 971.

[112] Whitman describes the schools in his study as "highly prescriptive institutions that often serve in loco parentis; they are morally and culturally assertive schools, which unapologetically insist that students adhere to middle-class virtues and explicitly rebuff the culture of the street; they are rigorous both about academics and instilling character; and they are places where obligation trumps freedom—they compel students to act according to school standards and preempt misbehavior, much in the manner of a watchful parent." WHITMAN, *supra* note 26, at 37.

[113] Scully, *supra* note 92, at 975.

[114] *Id.* at 975 ("The unequal use of zero tolerance policies can easily be attributed to conscious and/or unconscious racial bias. Teachers, administrators, and other school personnel who are prone to embracing stereotypes of Black children as unruly, out-of-control, or dangerous 'may react more quickly to relatively minor threats to authority.'").

[115] *Id.* at 989.

[116] *See generally* JABARI ASIM, NOT GUILTY: TWELVE BLACK MEN SPEAK OUT ON LAW, JUSTICE, AND LIFE (2001) (containing several essays from Black men on how their identity shaped their experience with law enforcement, the criminal justice system, and the educational system).

This risk is compounded when Black and Latino youth have been suspended out-of-school or expelled for trivial reasons.[117]

Codes of Conduct: Unfair Rules?

Charter school codes of conduct (also known as parent and student handbooks) should be clear and concise, especially when the schools employ punitive disciplinary practices. But after analyzing fifty-six charter school codes of conduct in Philadelphia for the 2014-2015 school year, Kerrin Wolf et. al. concluded that the codes varied considerably in quality and in philosophical approach to discipline.[118] Some common issues emerged in Wolf's study: many of the codes were not easily accessible to families online or in the home language of the student; some codes were vague and used overbroad terms without definition and so lacked clarity—the result of poor drafting; other codes emphasized the almost unchecked discretion of administrators to discipline students; yet other codes used very punitive language and terms that appear overly rigid; and most codes underscored shaming as a disciplinary response.[119]

For this paper, two codes of conduct are under consideration: one from City on a Hill Charter[120] and the other from Roxbury Prep.[121] Similar to the codes in Wolf's analysis, these

---

[117] Wolf et al., *supra* note 10.

[118] *Id.*

[119] *Id.*

[120] *Student Handbook*, CITY ON A HILL CHARTER SCH., http://www.cityonahill.org/wp-content/uploads/2015/11/Dudley-Student-Handbook-15-16-.pdf (last visited Jun. 4, 2016). Citations to the Handbook are omitted throughout the section.

[121] *Student & Family Handbook*, ROXBURY PREPARATORY CHARTER SCH., http://roxburyprep.uncommonschools.org/sites/default/files/downloads/student_handbook

two Codes differ in quality and depth, but both share basic tenets, such as vagueness and ambiguity in some of the language, the use of punitive (and even penal) language, and the granting of total discretion to school administrators (school leaders) to determine student discipline outcomes. Both also include a section on due process, pursuant to *Mass. Gen. Laws* ch. 71 § 37H¾ ,[122] for both short-term (less than ten days) and long-term (more than ten days) out-of-school suspensions.

City on a Hill Charter's Code of Conduct

Compared to Roxbury Prep's Code, City on a Hill's Code is much more detailed regarding offenses and consequences. Yet the code explicitly issues a caveat, namely that its list does not reflect all the behaviors subject to discipline. And ultimately, the "Deans' Office reserves the right to assign a behavior to an Offense Level and then assign a consequence." This is consistent with Wolf's assertion that most charter codes of conduct assign to the administrators "total or near total discretion" to determine the offense and the punishment.[123]

City on a Hill lists offenses as fitting within three levels, with each subsequent level more severe than the last. Level one refers to minor disruptions, level two to serious disruptions, and level three to "criminal, threatening, or dangerous behav-

---

 2015-16 updated.pdf (last visited Jun. 4, 2016). Citations to the Handbook are omitted throughout the section.

[122] *Mass. Gen. Laws* ch. 71 § 37H¾ (2014).

[123] Wolf et al., *supra* note 10, at 26.

iors."[124] Consequences for Level 1 Offenses include demerits, detentions, double detention, or a call home; for Level 2, the consequences include the same as Level 1 plus Deans/Principal meeting, student sent home, or suspension. The table's terminology (i.e. "level offenses") and organization resemble the Sentencing Table of the United States Sentencing Commission.[125] The Commission's Sentencing Table also includes a Criminal History Category, where Criminal History Points are matched with the offense level to determine the punishment.[126]

City on a Hill uses a merit/demerit system. Demerits, according to the Code, are "negative behavior points that are given for inappropriate behaviors" while merits "are positive behavior points that are given for positive behaviors that exemplify the school's expectations for students." The Code states that three or more demerits result in consequences for the student, with severity determined by the total number of demerits. Similarly, a convict receives a sentence determined by both the offense level and his or her Criminal History Points. It is unclear, however, how the demerits at City on a Hill intersect with the offense levels to determine a student's punishment. What is clear is that by using harsh penal terminology and the merit/demerit system (as used in military academies), the school shames students into occupying visible roles as ei-

---

[124] Since this paper deals only with Category 18 offenses, refer to Appendix II on page 54 for chart from City on a Hill's code for offenses considered non-drug, non-violent, non-criminal related offenses. Level 3 Offenses (not listed here) refer to violent behavior and to weapons and drug possession on campus.

[125] See Appendix III for Sentencing Table on page 55.

[126] *Sentencing Table*, UNITED STATES SENTENCING COMMISSION, http://www.ussc.gov/sites/default/files/pdf/guidelines-manual/2015/Sentencing_Table.pdf (last visited Jun. 29, 2016).

ther model conforming citizens or as deviant superpredators in need of severe punishment before they threaten the overall order of the school community.[127] Such codes reinforce to Black and Latino students that they are enemies in a system looking to exclude them for any and all offenses.[128]

Roxbury Prep's Code of Conduct

Roxbury Prep's Code clearly states that "students are held accountable through clear consequences for violating the school's rules." A reasonable parent would expect to see a clear table of offenses and corresponding punishments, or at the very least some description of how exactly administrators and teachers punish students. Instead parents and students can expect to find an arbitrary list of offenses (not meant to be exhaustive) with no corresponding consequences. The only guidance the Code offers is in the form of a sentence informing parents that

> [d]isciplinary offenses result in consequences subject to the discretion of the Principal, Director of Operations or their designee(s) and may include demerits, detention, school service/clearing, loss of school privileges, denial of school-provided transportation, Homework Center, Saturday School, extended detention, in-school suspension, short-term or long-term out-of-school suspension, and/or expulsion....

---

[127] WHITMAN, *supra* note 26, at 3 ("[N]ew paternalistic schools go further than even strict Catholic schools in prescribing student conduct and minimizing signs of disorder.").

[128] Scully, *supra* note 92, at 988 (noting that children and adolescents generally perceive "both blatant and subtle messages in their environment.").

Not only does this give administrators wide discretion to create offense categories and consequent punishments,[129] but it also fails to provide parents and students with a clear guideline of how discipline is enforced. The Code continues by noting that repeated infractions may result in suspension. These "repeated infractions" are neither defined nor detailed. These vague and overbroad terms are the result of poor drafting.[130] The Code promises to hold students "accountable through clear consequences," and yet parents and students will struggle to find what those clear consequences actually are.

For a school that suspended Black and Latino students for minor offenses at the highest rate in Massachusetts, the school administrators should consider drafting clearer rules of conduct with exact offenses and clear consequences for those offenses.

Due Process in Both Codes: Really or Not?

As a positive, both Codes list a similar due process procedure (as set forth in Mass. Gen. Laws ch. 71 § 37H¾) for short-term and long-term out-of-school suspensions.[131] Students receive an opportunity to participate in an informal hearing for short-term out-of-school suspensions. For these suspensions of ten days or less, the procedure requires that the school send a notice to the student and parent in English or

---

[129] Further complicating matters is the provision in the Code that allows staff members to assign "an appropriate consequence" for an offense, and staff members may then refer the matter to a school leader, who may then elect to review the offense and punishment and choose to take additional action.

[130] Wolf et al., *supra* note 10, at 33.

[131] *Mass. Gen. Laws* ch. 71 § 37H¾ (2014).

the primary language at home. The notice includes information about the "charge" along with the date, time, and location of the hearing. The principal must make a good-faith effort to contact the student's parent at least twice, so that the parent can understand what is occurring with the child.

The school must provide a hearing where the student is presented with the basis for the charge, along with facts regarding the offense. At this hearing, the student will have the opportunity to present information, such as mitigating facts for the principal to consider when deciding the punishment. Lastly, the school administrator must send his or her decision to the student and parent. The decision should outline the reason for the decision, the length of suspension, and any relevant schoolwork information. For long-term out-of-school suspensions, the procedure is the same as for short-term suspensions, but with more detail expected regarding the decision to suspend the student. Also, the student (not the parent) is given a right to appeal to the Executive Director of the school within five calendar days of the start of the suspension.

While guaranteeing due process to suspended students is a step forward, Wolf notes that most codes "presume that the formal hearing will result in punishment and does not contemplate the possibility that a student may not have committed an offense at all."[132] In other words, school administrators see these students (most of whom are Black and Latino) as an "out-of-control" group in need of surveillance and punishment even before they step into the classroom.[133] The superpredator

---

[132] Wolf et al., *supra* note 10, at 36.

[133] Scully, *supra* note 92, at 975-976 (arguing that the term out-of-control "is rampantly associated with Black and Brown children....").

myth advanced during the latter part of the 80s and early 90s seems to persist.

What does the U.S. Supreme Court and the Massachusetts Supreme Judicial Court have to say about school discipline? Do their rulings offer any hope for challenging exclusionary disciplinary methods that disproportionately affect so many Black and Latino youth?[134]

---

[134] *Id.*

PART II
Judicial Dance Around Student Rights

*G*iven past judicial holdings on school discipline, the prospect of the courts curbing the disproportionate application of exclusionary disciplinary policies does not seem promising. Even the most favorable decision regarding student rights in schools affords only minimal protection to students' due process rights.[135] Indeed, Justice Powell's dissent in *Goss* wondered whether the minimal due process protections the court granted students "will assure in any meaningful sense greater protection than that already afforded under Ohio law."[136] Justice Powell's skepticism stemmed from his fear of judicial encroachment on the educational arena.[137] Other justices have echoed Justice Powell's fear—and the Massachusetts Superior and Supreme Courts have even explicitly stated that courts should not interfere with school discipline or school matters generally.[138] This is just one

---

[135] *See Goss v. Lopez*, 419 U.S. 565 (1975).

[136] *Goss v. Lopez*, 419 U.S. 565, 597 (1975) (Powell, J., dissenting).

[137] *Id.*

[138] See *Doe v. Superintendent of Schs. of Stoughton*, 437 Mass 1 (2002); *Parkins v. Boule*, 2 Mass L. Rep. 331 (1994).

of a few commonalities the courts seem to share regarding student rights in schools.

The five cases[139] discussed here all reflect other common themes, such as: the importance of education for the state, but also the fact that education is not an absolute interest; the reluctance to overturn disciplinary decisions made by school officials; the preoccupation that school discipline will become inefficient with the introduction of more due process rights and other formal disciplinary and hearing procedures for students; the insistence that children and adults are entitled to different levels of rights; and the deference to school teachers and administrators in deciding and enforcing disciplinary policies. Even in the *Goss* decision, the majority noted that State and school authorities had wide discretion in setting and enforcing disciplinary standards.[140] The courts seem to be skirting around the issues, dancing around the rights of students. The judiciary hesitates to side with the student, especially Black and Latino students. Could *Brown's* philosophical vision provide a starting point?

Brown v. Board of Education (1954)

Historians, educators, and policymakers cite *Brown* as perhaps the most seminal education-related Supreme Court decision in U.S. history—and indeed, among the most impor-

---

[139] The cases include three Supreme Court cases: Brown v. Bd. of Educ., 347 U.S. 483 (1954); *Goss v. Lopez*, 419 U.S. 565 (1975); and N.J. v. T.L.O., 469 U.S. 325 (1985); and two Massachusetts cases: *Doe v. Superintendent of Schs. of Stoughton*, 437 Mass 1 (2002); and *Parkins v. Boule*, 2 Mass L. Rep. 331 (1994).

[140] *Goss*, 419 U.S. at 574.

tant in civil rights history.[141] With a tone of hope, Chief Justice Warren wrote that the doctrine of "separate but equal" was not valid under the U.S. Constitution, so the Court held that educating Black and white children in separate buildings was "inherently unequal."[142] But in the same opinion, Justice Warren also mentioned that "[t]o separate [Black children] from others of similar age and qualifications solely because of their race generates a feeling of inferiority as to their status in the community that may affect their hearts and minds in a way unlikely ever to be undone."[143] The *Brown* Court focused on the negative effects of segregation on only Black children; white children, according to the Court, seemed not to suffer any ill effects from never sharing a classroom or school with Black children. Further, the Court also seemed to imply that only Black children benefited from engagement with white children, but not the other way around.[144]

The *Brown* Court, however, did acknowledge the importance of education to the lives of all children. The Court noted that children who were denied education could not be expected to succeed personally and professionally in an increasingly technocratic civilization. The State thus was responsible for making education available to all children on equal grounds.[145]

---

[141] JAMES T. PATTERSON, BROWN V. BOARD OF EDUCATION: A CIVIL RIGHTS MILESTONE AND ITS TROUBLED LEGACY xiii-xiv (2001) (describing the excitement expressed by progressive news outlets and leaders of the African-American community after the Warren Court announced its unanimous decision).

[142] *Brown v. Bd. of Educ.*, 347 U.S. 483, 495 (1954).

[143] *Id.* at 494.

[144] BELL, *supra* note 13, at 196 ("[T]he unintended but readily assimilated side effect of that argument [that Black children were harmed by not coming into contact with white children] was that whites were not harmed, and their dominant position in all things important was right, just, and appropriate.").

[145] *Brown*, 347 U.S. at 493.

Bell and other scholars note that despite the seemingly reform-ist, progressive, and hope-filled rhetoric of the *Brown* Court, implementation of the *Brown* ideals has failed.[146] For instance, a decade after *Brown*, roughly only 1.2% of all Black students in the old Confederate states actually enrolled in public schools with white children.[147] There was also white flight from schools, leaving Black children perhaps in a worse socioeco-nomic position than they had been when they were educated in their own schools by teachers who looked like the students.[148]

Further, Bell notes that "[e]quality by proclamation not only failed to truly reflect the complexity of racial subordina-tion, it also vested the government and the courts with the ul-timate moral authority to define African-American freedom."[149] Hence, even the most foundational Court decision for equal education and student rights is riddled with internal contradic-tions and problems with its application. The alleged failure of *Brown* to galvanize local educators to provide an equal educa-tion to all children serves as a reminder that judicial decisions––even when seemingly geared toward reform—may either not be enforced at the local level or may have worse consequences than the harm it was trying to eliminate.[150]

---

[146] BELL, *supra* note 13, at 196.

[147] PATTERSON, *supra* note 141.

[148] *Id.*

[149] BELL, *supra* note 13, at 186.

[150] PATTERSON, *supra* note 141. Patterson, however, notes that *Brown* may have encour-aged northern states to enact laws banning racial discrimination in employment and housing. *Id.*

Goss v. Lopez (1975)

Civil rights lawyers concerned with student rights often cite *Goss* for support, particularly regarding due process rights.[151] In *Goss*, school administrators suspended seventy-five students for the same incident in the school cafeteria. The Court noted that school administrators never held hearings for the suspended students.[152] So the *Goss* Court affirmed the Ohio court's holding that the students "were denied due process of law because they were suspended without a hearing prior to suspension or within a reasonable time thereafter...."[153] The *Goss* Court dismissed appellant's argument that, since there is no constitutional right to education, the Due Process Clause should not protect against suspensions or expulsions from the public school system.[154] The Court noted that Ohio law and statues—especially the one requiring attendance—entitled all children to an education.[155] The Court also reaffirmed an earlier holding that students did not "shed their constitutional rights" upon entering a school.[156]

Next the Court argued that "[t]he Due Process Clause also forbids arbitrary deprivations of liberty," especially when it concerns a person's reputation and sense of honor before the

---

[151] See *Student Discipline Rights and Procedures: A Guide for Advocates*, EDUCATION LAW CENTER, http://www.edlawcenter.org/assets/files/pdfs/publications/StudentDisciplineRights_Guide_2012.pdf (last accessed Aug. 4, 2016).

[152] *Goss v. Lopez*, 419 U.S. 565, 571 (1975).

[153] *Id.* at 571.

[154] *Id.*

[155] *Id.* at 574 ("Although Ohio may not be constitutionally obligated to establish and maintain a public school system, it has nevertheless done so and has required its children to attend.").

[156] *Tinker v. Des Moines School Dist.*, 393 U.S. 503, 506 (1969).

community.[157] Suspending students for up to ten days, the Court wrote, "could seriously damage the students' standing with their fellow pupils and their teachers as well as interfere with later opportunities for higher education and employment."[158] Hence, the Court refuted the appellant's argument that a ten-day suspension is far milder than expulsion and so inconsequential in Due Process concerns.[159] On the contrary, the Court argued that suspension for ten days "is a serious event in the life of a suspended child" because a suspension denies the suspended child access to the state's most important function, education.[160] The Court's acknowledgment of the negative effects of suspensions is commendable, especially when considering the decision's date: 1975. Had these justices been around today, they would have noted the perilous consequences of exclusionary discipline, especially for Black and Latino youth.[161]

But the *Goss* Court issued several caveats and limitations. First, the Court reaffirmed its earlier admonition against judicial overreach into the operation of the public schools: "By and large, public education in our Nation is committed to the control of state and local authorities."[162] The opinion also noted that although the State's authority to set and enforce disciplinary standards was very broad, such authority must nonetheless "be exercised consistently with constitutional safe-

---

[157] *Goss*, 419 U.S. at 574.

[158] *Id.* at 575.

[159] *Goss*, 419 U.S. at 575.

[160] *Id.* at 576.

[161] Scully, *supra* note 92 (noting the various serious consequences of exclusionary discipline on Black and Latino students, including the school-to-prison pipeline).

[162] *Epperson v. Arkansas*, 393 U.S. 97, 104 (1968).

guards."[163] Once again the Court danced around the issue—it simultaneously acknowledged educators' wide discretion to set conduct policies while also advocating for that discretion to occur within constitutional confines.

The Court then raised the issue of disciplinary efficiency,[164] and the role of suspensions as "a valuable educational device."[165] Hence it did not advocate limiting suspensions or holding intricate hearings each time a student is suspended; it merely called for schools to provide students with "*some* kind of notice and … *some* kind of hearing."[166] What these notices and hearings entailed is not clear from the decision. It seemed the Court required "at least an informal give-and-take between student and disciplinarian" following the alleged misconduct and "preferably before the suspension."[167] This informal encounter did not require that schools provide students with the right to secure counsel, to confront the accuser or to cross-examine witnesses, or even to call his or her own witnesses.[168] Again, the Court left wide discretion for educators and local officials to determine exactly what these minimal Due Process requirements entailed. The *Goss* decision results in different criteria for suspensions among the different schools, leaving some students more vulnerable than others to arbitrary disciplinary decisions.

---

[163] *Goss*, 419 U.S. at 574.

[164] *See Id.* at 583 ("Brief disciplinary suspensions are almost countless. To impose in each such case even truncated trial-type procedures might well overwhelm administrative faculties in many places and, by diverting resources, cost more than it would save in educational effectiveness.").

[165] *Id.* at 580 (1975).

[166] *Id.* at 579.

[167] *Id.* at 584.

[168] *Id.*

Thus, even the most favorable opinion for student rights activists acknowledged judicial constraint in imposing stringent standards or limitations on the application of discipline in public schools. Ultimately, the *Goss* Court left discipline decisions up to educators and local officials; they are to decide what is required in disciplinary hearings beyond the *Goss* court's bare bones requirements.[169]

N.J. v. T.L.O (1985)

This case considered the scope of searches and seizures in public schools. Two girls were caught smoking cigarettes in a school bathroom. The school's Vice Principal ("VP") suspected that one of the girls carried cigarettes in her purse—a clear violation of the school's anti-smoking policy. The VP searched the girl's purse and found cigarettes, along with some rolling paper. He inferred from this that the girl could be in possession of more than just cigarettes, so he conducted a more thorough search of the purse. The VP then found a pipe, bags to package marihuana, a small amount of marihuana, and an index card containing a list of people who owed the girl money. The evidence led the VP to believe the girl was selling and distributing drugs in school.[170] The Supreme Court of New Jersey reversed the Appellate Division's judgment and ordered the suppression of all evidence in the girl's purse.[171] The court noted that the search violated the Fourth Amendment and so rendered the evidence inadmissible.[172] The Supreme Court,

---

[169] *Id.*

[170] *N.J. v. T.L.O.*, 469 U.S. 325 (1985).

[171] *Id.*

[172] *Id.*

however, reversed and held the search and seizure reasonable under the circumstances.

First, the Court held that public school officials were agents of the state, not surrogate parents, and thus were not immune from constitutional constraints.[173] As agents of the state, educators should teach through example the "scrupulous protection of Constitutional freedoms of the individual" or risk students perceiving Constitutional principles "as mere platitudes."[174] Indeed, teaching through example is essential to students, but if students perceive that disciplinary policies are unfairly and arbitrary applied, they may discount authority as fundamentally unjust.[175]

Second, the Court followed its decision in *Goss* and acknowledged that educators must have flexibility to exercise discretion in order to preserve a safe and secure learning environment.[176] Thus, the opinion advocated for the continuation of the informal student-teacher relationship.[177] The Court lamented that ensuring discipline and order was growing more difficult in recent years, since "school disorder has often taken particularly ugly forms: drug use and violent in the schools have become major social problems."[178] This reflects the social anxiety created and promoted by the media's image of out-of-

---

[173] *Id.* at 336 ("[T]oday's public school officials do not merely exercise authority voluntarily conferred on them by individual parents; rather, they act in furtherance of publically mandated educational and disciplinary policies."). The Court also notes that school officials have been held subject to the First Amendment and to Fourteenth Amendment of the Due Process Clause.

[174] *Id.* at 334.

[175] *See* Wolf et al., *supra* note 10.

[176] *T.L.O.*, 469 U.S.

[177] *Id.*

[178] *Id.* at 339.

control, violent youth during the 80s.[179] Even the Court was susceptible to the myth of the superpredators. Thus, the Court was unwilling to require warrants for searches, since educators needed to take swift action to prevent dangerous children from enacting nefarious plots in schools.[180]

Third, the Court was also unwilling to extend the probable cause standard to students subjected to searches.[181] Instead, "the legality of the search of a student should depend simply on the reasonableness, under all the circumstances, of the search."[182] The Court relied on the *Terry* two-fold test to determine reasonableness: 1) whether the search was justified at its inception; and 2) whether the search "was reasonably related in scope to the circumstances which justified the interference in the first place."[183] Focusing on the reasonableness standard, the Court argued, "will spare teachers and school administrators the necessity of schooling themselves in the niceties of probable cause and permit them to regulate their conduct according to the dictates of reason and common sense."[184] Again, efficiency and the discretion of the educators were considered more important than student rights.

Finally, this opinion contradicted itself: first it noted that teachers should be exemplars of Constitutional standards to students, and yet curiously these same teachers should be

---

[179] Scully, *supra* note 92.

[180] *T.L.O.*, 469 U.S. at 340 ("[T]he warrant requirement, in particular, is unsuited to the school environment: requiring a teacher to obtain a warrant before searching a child suspected of an infraction of school rules (or of the criminal law) would unduly interfere with the maintenance of the swift and informal disciplinary procedures needed in the schools.").

[181] *Id.*

[182] *Id.* at 341.

[183] *Terry v. Ohio*, 392 U.S. 1, 20 (1968).

[184] *T.L.O.*, 469 U.S. at 344.

"spared" educating themselves on Constitutional standards.[185] Also, the Court seemed to infer that all educators were usually reasonable, and so it did not hesitate to acknowledge that ordinarily a student search by an educator would be "justified at its inception."[186] This precludes the possibility that educators may be acting unreasonably when they allow their racial biases (whether explicit or implicit) to influence their discipline of Black and Latino students.[187] According to Powell's concurring opinion, students should simply not be granted the same constitutional protections as adults.[188] Clearly, *stare decisis* is not on the side of student rights. Precedent favors allotting wide discretion to the reasonable educator to set and enforce disciplinary policies—all under the guise of efficiency and school safety.

Doe v. Superintendent of Schools of Stoughton (2002)

This Massachusetts Supreme Judicial Court decision bears several similarities to the Supreme Court decisions just discussed. In *Doe*, a high school principal suspended a student after the principal learned from authorities that the student had been charged with battery, rape and abuse of a boy under four-

---

[185] Justice Brennan underscored the contradiction in his dissent: "[I]t would be incongruous and futile to charge teachers with the task of imbuing their students with an understanding of our system of constitutional democracy, while at the same time immunizing those same teachers from the need to respect constitutional protections. *T.L.O.*, 469 U.S. at 354. In his dissent, Justice Stevens remarked that "the Court's decision today is a curious moral for the Nation's youth. Although the search of T.L.O.'s purse does not trouble today's majority, I submit that we are not dealing with 'matters relatively trivial to the welfare of the Nation. There are village tyrants as well as village Hampdens, but none who acts under color of law is beyond reach of the Constitution.'" *T.L.O.*, 469 U.S. at 386.

[186] *Terry v. Ohio*, 392 U.S. 1, 19 (1968).

[187] Scully, *supra* note 92.

[188] *T.L.O.*, 469 U.S. (Powell, J., concurring).

teen years old.[189] The district's superintendent affirmed the principal's decision, and the suspended student appealed the suspension in court. The Superior Court held that the superintendent abused his discretion by suspending the student when there was "no evidence that [the student's] presence at the school had any negative effect on the school population."[190] The Supreme Judicial Court, however, reversed the lower court's ruling and upheld the principal's and superintendent's decision to suspend the student from school because of their rational belief that the student presented a viable threat to the student population, especially to elementary and middle-school students.[191]

The court noted that although it had never decided the standard of review for a superintendent's decision to suspend, courts in Massachusetts "have always accorded school officials substantial deference in matters of discipline."[192] The opinion justified this "substantial deference" to school officials by highlighting that school officials "are in the best position to determine when a student's actions threaten the safety and welfare of other students...."[193] As with the Supreme Court decisions, the court here continued to grant educators wide discretion in enforcing disciplinary policies—a holding which is also in line with Massachusetts judicial precedent.[194]

---

[189] The student allegedly admitted to sodomizing the young boy in a garage with his finger and a pipe. He then described the entire incident as a joke. *Doe v. Superintendent of Schs. of Stoughton*, 437 Mass 1 (2002).

[190] *Id.* at 4.

[191] *Id.*

[192] *Id.* at 5.

[193] *Id.*

[194] *Leonard v. School Comm. of Attleboro*, 349 Mass. 704, 709 (1965) ("School committees have wide discretion in school discipline matters.").

Next the court stated that it would only overturn a superintendent's decision when that decision to suspend a student "is arbitrary and capricious, so as to constitute an abuse of discretion."[195] According to the court, a decision is arbitrary and capricious if reasonable persons cannot agree on the rationale given for the decision.[196] As in *T.L.O.*, the reasonable person standard again surfaced, and as with *T.L.O.*, one can infer that most courts will view teachers and schools administrators as more reasonable than students. Students are simply on the losing end of judicial decisions that apply the reasonable person standard to gauge whether disciplinary decisions were just.

Yet, the Massachusetts Supreme Judicial Court went farther by warning that "[i]t is not the place of a reviewing court to substitute its own opinion for that of a superintendent."[197] Not only will a student have a difficult time proving the school administrator's decision was unreasonable, but this court erected an almost impenetrable shield around each and every decision by superintendents and principals, as long as the decisions appear rational to reasonable minds.[198] Further complicating matters is the question of whom the court considers a reasonable person. Is it a white male educator or school official? The standard's vagueness serves as a safeguard that allows principals and other school officials to exercise their legal discretion to discipline students as they see fit—with little inter-

---

[195] *Superintendent of Schs. of Stoughton*, 437 Mass at 5.

[196] *Id.*

[197] *Id.* at 6.

[198] *Id.*

ference from the courts. Do the lower courts in Massachusetts fare any better?

Parkins v. Boule (1994)

In this case before the trial court, a 15-year-old girl brought a small knife (lipstick knife) to school to show her friends. Her mother's boyfriend gave her the knife as a gift, and due to the knife's small size, the girl thought the gift was a joke.[199] The school's principal considered the lipstick-style knife a dangerous weapon and so expelled the student. The principal felt the student was a threat to school safety, regardless of whether she intended to use the knife.[200] The district superintendent believed there was no difference between a weapon and a dangerous weapon. Weapons of any sort, he thought, were weapons that could threaten a learning environment—and so he upheld the principal's decision to expel the student.[201] The court affirmed the superintendent's decision, citing his experience and the rational explanation for his decision.

The court's reasoning, no surprise, mimics the decisions of the Supreme Court, especially *T.L.O.*, and of the Massachusetts Supreme Judicial Court. First, the court acknowledged the standard in Massachusetts, that is, whether the disciplinary decision was arbitrary and capricious and so an abuse of discretion.[202] Compared to the *Doe v. Superintendent of Schs. of Stoughton* decision, this court sets an even less stringent standard in de-

---

[199] *Parkins v. Boule*, 2 Mass L. Rep. 331 (1994).

[200] The principal considered any knife-like object (regardless of size) a dangerous weapon. *Id.*

[201] *Id.*

[202] *Id.*

termining what constitutes an arbitrary and capricious decision by stating that the standards "require only that there be a rational basis for decision...."[203]

This leaves the door wide open for educators to justify their decisions to apply exclusionary discipline, especially if these educators have extensive experience in education.[204] Indeed, in the opinion, the court highlighted the educators' extensive years of experience in the public schools.[205] The court thus inferred that more professional experience translated into automatic rational and reasonable decisions by educators. This added layer of deference to more experienced educators, coupled with historical judicial reluctance to encroach on disciplinary matters in the public schools, has left students and their advocates with very little recourse to address unjust suspensions in the courts.[206] This court even went as far as to cite a Supreme Court case that stated "it is not for the courts to set aside decisions of school administrators which the Court may view as 'lacking a basis in wisdom or compassion.'"[207] Clearly, courts wish not to intervene in public school disciplinary matters, even if one or a few of the judges might feel the disciplinary decision lacked compassion for the student.

---

[203] *Id.* at 337.

[204] *Id.* (considering the principal's eight years experience as assistant principal).

[205] *Id.*

[206] *Id.*

[207] *Wood v. Strickland*, 420 U.S. 308, 326 (1975).

Matters are more complicated when one considers that the majority of the cases discussed above dealt with students suspended or expelled for more serious offenses, such as for drug, violent, and/or criminal-related offenses. This paper addresses only Category 18 offenses—offenses that may be considered even too trivial to bring to the court's attention. The courts may dismiss any student claims of arbitrary and capricious suspensions as better handled within the school itself or by the local district instead of in the courts. Judges might fear a flood of "frivolous" litigation concerning student suspensions for passing gas, writing on the desk, or skipping class.

Since the history of student rights litigation shows that courts are at best only willing to provide students with very minimal protections, what are the choices for student rights activists seeking to address the serious consequences of disparate suspensions of Black and Latino youth in Massachusetts—and, indeed, in the nation's—charter schools? Clearly the courts are not the place to effectuate efficacious change to the application of exclusionary disciplinary practices. But there is hope—once activists decide not to tango with the courts.

PART III

Hope of Reform: Chapter 222 as a Start, Restorative Justice, School Culture, and Grassroots

*T*he disparate application of exclusionary disciplinary policies on Black and Latino youth and the concomitant risk of these same students falling into the vicious school-to-prison pipeline should concern the entire nation. Indeed, one scholar sees dismantling the school-to-prison pipeline "[a]s one of the most important civil rights issues of the twenty-first century...."[208] And as this paper has shown, the issue of disparate student suspensions is very complex with multifaceted consequences for Black and Latino youth. The responses to exclusionary disciplinary policies and their disparate application will likewise be complex and multi-faceted.[209] Effective responses will require the concentrated efforts of students, parents, school administrators, teachers, lawyers, policymakers, grassroots organizations, research professors, and student rights activists.[210] But above all, the solution requires a reorientation of educational philosophy and teacher training.

---

[208] Scully, *supra* note 92, at 962.

[209] *Id.*

[210] *Id.*

Philosophical Reorientation:
The Most Vital Ingredient

In addition to strategic responses, a philosophical change is essential to any reform. Viewing Black and Latino children as difficult, out-of-control, violence-prone superpredators who require tough discipline is neither correct nor ethical.[211] The public in general, and educators in particular, need to confront their biases and receive the appropriate training to reorient their flawed and racist worldviews.[212] Thus, undergraduate and graduate programs in education—particularly those programs geared toward "urban" education—should offer courses specifically addressing education and race. At the very least, schools should offer educators intensive professional training sessions focused on critical race theory.[213]

Teachers and school administrators, in dealing with diverse children, have an ethical calling to attempt to understand their students' backgrounds, cultures, and home/neighborhood situation.[214] The legislature should offer financial incentives to

---

[211] *See, e.g.,* ANGELA VALENZUELA, SUBTRACTIVE SCHOOLING: U.S.-MEXICAN YOUTH AND THE POLITICS OF CARING 62 (1999) (addressing how educators—especially white educators—discount the lived experiences and cultures of Latino students).

[212] Scully, *supra* note 92.

[213] A useful and succinct book I used during faculty and student training sessions at an all-boys high school I taught at in Boston is RICHARD DELGADO & JEAN STEFANCIC, CRITICAL RACE THEORY: AN INTRODUCTION (2012). Most educators feel overwhelmed with their current time commitments, so a short, solid book will be useful for professional training sessions in lieu of more complicated, scholarly treaties on the subject. Teachers interested in mastering critical race theory can consult the more in-depth material individually and then present summaries to the faculty at meetings or in small reading groups. Strategies will vary depending on the vision and energy of the principal and teacher leaders.

[214] Scully, *supra* note 92, at 969 (noting that in Texas, School Resource Officers (SROs) are required to participate in biannual training on a range of relevant topics, such as "child development and psychology, cultural competence, restorative justice techniques, accommodating students with disabilities, and creation of safe spaces for LGBTQ students."). Schools should implement a similar type of required training for teachers and school administrators at certain

schools that hire and retain faculty with extensive training in cultural competence, critical race theory, and disability studies.[215] These same faculty could then train other faculty at the school, thereby reducing the costs associated with bringing external educators to train the entire school faculty. Lastly, public and charter schools should consider hiring more Black and Latino teachers, since studies show that children and adolescents respond better to an educator who looks like them.[216] These educators could also bring to the school a multicultural perspective that could prove insightful to other faculty and staff.

Sample of Strategic Responses

Apart from philosophical reorientation, this paper proposes three strategic solutions for curbing disparate suspensions and dismantling the school-to-prison pipeline: 1) progressive legislation such as Chapter 222; 2) restorative discipline as an alternative to punitive, exclusionary discipline; and 3) the need for grassroots organizations and student rights activists to monitor the implementation of legislation and student discipline in schools. These are only but a few of the possible responses to the issue. Any response, however, must flow the

---

periods: before the start of each school year, before school resumes in January, and when the school year ends. Such regular training will also allow school officials to assess the application of disciplinary policies.

[215] Scully, *supra* note 92 (arguing that the legislature should relieve some tax burdens at schools which implement more progressive disciplinary polices). Similarly, the legislature should provide financial incentives to schools that hire and retain faculty specialized in the areas mentioned.

[216] *See* GLORIA LADSON-BILLINGS, THE DREAMKEEPERS: SUCCESSFUL TEACHERS OF AFRICAN-AMERICAN CHILDREN (1994).

philosophical reorientation discussed above, or the responses risk leading to unintended negative consequences.[217]

Chapter 222 as a Start

Rep. Alice Wolf from Cambridge introduced Chapter 222 as House Bill 4332 in 2011.[218] The legislature approved Chapter 222 on August 6, 2012, with the law taking effect on July 1, 2014.[219] Chapter 222 was the result of grassroots organizations concerned over exclusionary disciplinary policies, their application, and their consequences.[220] Governor Deval Patrick allocated funds for the implementation of Chapter 222 in the 2015 Massachusetts Budget.[221] Massachusetts clearly sought to regulate disciplinary procedures, and one scholar even believes that Chapter 222 calls for restorative justice since it requires that school officials use exclusionary discipline only as a last resort, after they have exhausted all other methods.[222]

---

[217] In the U.S., there is a persistent problem: expanding new programs before we know if they work, and how successes might be replicated on a larger scale. This is the case with the charter school movement and with the many reform movements before it. Reformers, educators, and policymakers need to carefully consider all the options. But if one is to address educational inequality, one needs to address the multiple inequalities in society. KEVIN K. KUMASHIRO, THE SEDUCTION OF COMMON SENSE: HOW THE RIGHT HAS FRAMED THE DEBATE ON AMERICA'S SCHOOLS 97 (2008) ("[Q]uality education is a right for all people, but because schools do not exist in a vacuum, advocating for education rights must intersect with advocacy for political, economic, social, developmental, and environmental rights.").

[218] The Bill's title was "An Act Relative to Students' Access to Educational Services and Exclusion from School."

[219] *How We Won School Discipline Reform in Massachusetts*, SCHOTT FOUND. FOR PUB. EDUC. REFORM BLOG, http://schottfoundation.org/blog/2014/07/23/how-we-won-school-discipline-reform-massachusetts (last visited Jun. 19, 2016).

[220] *Id.*

[221] *Id.*

[222] Though Chapter 222 does not mention restorative justice, one can infer that the Act urges school officials to try alternative disciplinary methods, such as restorative justice, before resorting to suspensions and/or expulsions. *See* Armour, *supra* note 17.

Indeed, Chapter 222 introduces three important subsections to Section 37H (Student Conduct) of Chapter 71 (Public Schools) of the Massachusetts General Laws.[223]

Subsection (e) requires that school districts provide suspended or expelled students with continuation of educational services.[224] And if that student moves to another district while suspended or after expulsion, the new district must "either admit the student to its schools or provide educational services to the student in an education service plan...."[225] This is a vast improvement over past practices, when school districts had no obligation to continue providing suspended or expelled students any services, and when other districts had discretion as to whether accept the student in its schools.[226]

Subsection (f) establishes the requirements for data collection and accountability.[227] The subsection requires that districts report to the Department of Elementary and Secondary Education the specific reasons for every type of suspension and expulsion, including short-term suspensions. The department of elementary and secondary education must then collect and breakdown the data by school districts and student demographics; the data must then be made available online to the general public. The education commissioner establishes the categories.[228]

---

[223] *Mass. Gen. Laws* ch. 71, §37H (2014).

[224] *Mass. Gen. Laws* ch. 71, §37H (e).

[225] *Id.*

[226] Jarboe, *supra* note 56.

[227] *Mass. Gen. Laws* ch. 71, §37H (f).

[228] *Id.*

Subsection (f) is highly commendable for two reasons: 1) it allows researchers and grassroots organizations to examine the suspension and expulsion trends according to student demographics, such as race, socioeconomic status, gender, and disability; and 2) it allows schools to assess their rates of suspensions and expulsions in comparison to other similar schools. Further, the data collection, broken down by "offense" categories, allows the general public to see what students are disciplined for. As this paper has shown, trends do emerge from analyzing the data, namely that charter schools suspended more often than public schools, and that Black and Latino males (as well as students with disabilities) were disproportionately suspended out-of-school for non-drug, non-violent, non-criminal related offenses.

The data would be even more useful, however, if it broke down out-of-school suspensions into two other categories: those exceeding ten days and those not exceeding ten days. The data should also reflect what specific offenses students were suspended for under the broad umbrella of Category 18 offenses. Lastly, the data should specify whether student statuses overlap; for instance, how many students with disabilities are also Latino or female? Or how many poor students are also Black or white or male? Long term, it would also be helpful to learn how students and parents chose their identities for data collection. These suggestions would make the data that much more effective for purposes of research, assessment, and accountability regarding the implementation of Chapter 222.

Subsection (g) allows the commissioner of education to investigate any school that "suspends or expels a significant number of students for more than 10 cumulative days in a school year."[229] After investigating the school, the commissioner must then offer the school recommendations to ensure that suspensions and expulsions are truly a last resort.[230] All analyses will be reported publicly within the school district.[231] This accountability measure is crucial because it will undoubtedly pressure school officials to handle disciplinary matters with more discretion. Schools will want to be spared the embarrassment of being singled out by the commissioner for excessively suspending or expelling students, especially if the students are of color or disabled. By publishing the results at the district level, parents and others will be able to make a more informed choice of whether to send their children to a school that expels without resorting to other measures first.

i. Section 37H¾

Regarding student discipline and conduct, Chapter 222, in subsection § 37H¾, requires that all school administrators use discretion when contemplating whether to suspend or expel a student. Further, school officials must "consider ways to reengage the student in the learning process," and must use exclusionary discipline only as a last resort.[232]

Subsection (c) affords more protection to students' notice and due process rights than did the *Goss* decision.[233] Whereas *Goss* held that only suspensions of ten days or more might merit a formal notice and hearing process, subsection (c) requires that a notice accompany any type of suspension or

---

[229] *Mass. Gen. Laws* ch. 71, §37H (g).

[230] *Id.*

[231] *Id.*

[232] *Mass. Gen. Laws* ch. 71, §§37H¾ (2014).

[233] *Goss v. Lopez*, 419 U.S. 565 (1975).

expulsion. The notice must inform students and parents of the charges and the reason for the disciplinary decision.[234] Moreover, the student has the right to meet with the school official making the decision to discuss the charges and reason for suspension or expulsion before the suspension or expulsion takes effect.[235]

Subsection (d) requires schools to provide written notice to students and parents informing them of their right to appeal to school officials any suspensions or expulsions of more than ten consecutive or cumulative days in a school year.[236]

Subsection (e) provides students the right to appeal their suspension or expulsion to the district superintendent.[237] At this appeals hearing, a student's rights are extended beyond the protections in *Goss*.[238] The student "shall have the right to present oral and written testimony, cross-examine witnesses and shall have the right to counsel."[239] The students' ability to defend themselves against charges could provide a balance to the principal's absolute discretion. More importantly, students will develop agency and advocacy skills by participating in their own defense.[240]

All in all, Chapter 222 offers hope for a progressive stance toward school discipline. And its data collection and accountability measures provide opportunities for the public to

---

[234] Mass. Gen. Laws ch. 71, §§37H¾ (c).

[235] *Id.*

[236] *Mass. Gen. Laws* ch. 71, §§37H¾ (d).

[237] *Mass. Gen. Laws* ch. 71, §§37H¾ (e).

[238] *Goss v. Lopez,* 419 U.S. 565 (1975).

[239] *Mass. Gen. Laws* ch. 71, §37H¾ (e).

[240] Armour, *supra* note 17.

monitor whether Chapter 222's goal of reducing student suspensions is truly working. Under the requirements of Chapter 222, the commissioner of education should investigate both Roxbury Prep Charter and City on a Hill Charter in particular, and the rest of the Massachusetts charter school system in general. How is it possible that these schools suspended Black and Latino students at higher rates than the public schools for Category 18 offenses? Parents and grassroots organizations should demand an answer soon, especially with an upcoming ballot question that will determine whether charter schools will continue to expand in the Commonwealth. At the very least, Chapter 222 allows for data—rather than conjecture—to guide the conversation on school discipline.

Restorative Justice and Practices in the School Setting

Potential solutions to exclusionary discipline must include those beyond legislative confines. One commentator notes that relying on legislation to solve issues will result in confronting "disappointment of constant change due to the fluctuation of political will as the Legislature changes faces and ideologies."[241] One such non-legislative solution gaining traction across many states is restorative justice.[242] Restorative justice seeks to repair harm to relationships by restoring both the offender and the victim to right relationships in the community.[243] In contrast, punitive justice blames and punishes the

---

[241] Scully, *supra* note 92, at 1007.

[242] Although many states across the U.S. employ restorative practices, the following states are leading the way: California, Colorado, Georgia, Illinois, Maine, Maryland, Massachusetts, Michigan, Minnesota, Missouri, New York, Texas, Connecticut, and Pennsylvania. Armour, *supra* note 17, at 1016.

[243] Scully, *supra* note 92.

wrongdoer without necessarily addressing the causes of the offense or the consequences.[244] Restorative justice practices, at their core, "are predicated on the belief that when a violation occurs, it breaks human connections, throwing the entire community into disharmony."[245] Thus, a community using the restorative approach will seek to mend broken relationships by valuing respect for all community members, accountability, and the importance of strong relationships to personal growth and development.[246]

In school settings, restorative justice is often known as restorative practices.[247] To become effective, a school-based restorative practice will require input from students. The input will help educators develop practices that are context-specific.[248] By holding students accountable for their actions, and by including students in the process of implementation, school administrators will instill a sense of agency and, more importantly, belonging among the students.[249] This, in turn, will create a school-wide climate of mutual respect, active community building and participation, and truth telling—the cornerstones of democratic citizenship.[250] Restorative practices ask: "(1) what is the harm caused and to whom, (2) what are the needs and obligations that have arisen, and (3) who has the obligation to address the needs, to repair the harm, and to restore

---

[244] *Id.*

[245] Armour, *supra* note 17, at 1015.

[246] *Id.*

[247] Other names include Circles, Restorative Processes, Restorative Measures, Restorative Approaches, and Restorative Discipline. *Id.*

[248] *Id.* at 1017.

[249] *Id.* at 1016.

[250] *Id.* at 1016.

relationships."[251] A punitive model, in contrast, focuses on the rules broken, the offender, and the punishment.[252] The American Psychological Association's Zero Tolerance Task Force endorsed restorative practices as an alternative to exclusionary disciplinary policies because of its effectiveness in repairing broken relationships, reducing suspensions and expulsions, and teaching students relational and problem-solving skills.[253]

Some students even show positive results in the home context. In Oakland, students in restorative circles "reported enhanced ability to understand peers, manage emotions, demonstrate greater empathy, resolve conflicts with parents, [and] improve their home environments...."[254] Data suggest that restorative practices reduce suspensions and physical fights among students, while also improving student engagement in school life and academics.[255] More importantly, restorative practices also seem to reduce the disproportionate impact of exclusionary disciplinary policies on Black and Latino youth.[256]

---

[251] *Id.* at 1018.

[252] *Id.*

[253] Scully, *supra* note 92.

[254] Armour, *supra* note 17, at 1021.

[255] Though it is beyond the scope of this paper to delve into the quantitative effectiveness of restorative practices in schools, a comparative study of Oakland schools shows that "reading levels in grade 9 doubled in [restorative justice] high schools from an average of 14% to 33%, an increase of 128%, compared to 11% in [non- restorative justice] high schools. Moreover, from 2010-2013, [restorative justice] high schools experienced a 56% decline in high school dropout rates in comparison to 17% for [non-restorative justice] high schools. Graduation rates increased 60% over three years compared to 7% for non-restorative justice high schools." *Id.* at 1020-21.

[256] Two studies show promising results at schools that use restorative practice: 1) "A three-year study of restorative practices in a K-8 urban school found that out-of-school suspensions fell from 51% to 14% for African American students, 34% to 6% for Hispanic students, 39% to 6% for multiracial students, and 51% to 9% for white students"; and 2) "A study of school-based restorative justice in Oakland School District found a 40% decrease in the number of suspensions for African American students. Moreover, the discipline gap between black and white students had closed from 12.6% to 9.2% in the restorative justice schools compared to an increase in the control schools." *Id.* at 1022-23.

Restorative practices can therefore help dismantle the school-to-prison pipeline that is destroying communities and individuals by focusing on keeping students in schools rather than getting rid of them for minor infractions.

Yet there are some caveats. First, the idea of restorative practice is relatively fresh in educational circles, so currently there is no consensus regarding standards of implementation, how best to train teachers and school administrators, or how to design restorative practices corresponding to different grade levels.[257] Educators should work together with all school stakeholders in brainstorming ideas for design and implementation of restorative practices for particular contexts.

Second, research at schools that have implemented restorative practices shows that implementation is usually a three- to five-year process.[258] This means that swift implementation will likely fail, so educators and others must be patient and introduce restorative practices slowly, particularly in schools with many veteran teachers.[259] School districts and schools must avoid eliminating all traditional disciplinary methods all at once. Without strategic planning, adequate educator training, and methodically phasing out of traditional practices, restorative practices will not work in a system already wired to discipline in traditional ways.[260]

---

[257] *Id.*

[258] *Id.*

[259] *See generally* VIVIAN TROEN & KATHERINE BOLES, WHO'S TEACHING YOUR CHILDREN (2004) (articulating the need for better teacher training and advocating patience with veteran teachers who hold a conservative educational philosophy when enacting school reforms).

[260] *See* Armour, *supra* note 17, at 1030-1034 (presenting 13 best practices for the implementation of restorative practices).

Last, restorative justice is a term used within the criminal justice system. Reformers and even students might believe that philosophical reorientation has not occurred if this term is used. Students might think that educators—and society—still see them as naturally violent offenders instead of students in development.[261] Perhaps employing another term would be useful. Or educators could explain to students and parents that the roots of restorative justice actually stem from indigenous cultures who used restorative practices to heal the community's fractured relationships.[262] Situating restorative practices within Native American cultures—instead of within the criminal justice system—could help Black and Latino students see restorative practices as a holistic alternative to Western systems of punitive discipline, which they resist.[263]

Grassroots: Helping to Keep it Real

Ultimately, for any concrete, lasting reform to occur, communities and concerned citizens will need to hold schools and the legislature accountable for reforming exclusionary disciplinary policies.[264] Communities should form grassroots organizations dedicated to student rights. Naturally, such a coalition should include students, parents, progressive and visionary

---

[261] *Id.* at 1020-21.

[262] Scully, *supra* note 92, 998.

[263] *See* MICHEL FOUCAULT, DISCIPLINE AND PUNISH: THE BIRTH OF THE PRISON 183 (1975) ("[T]he perpetual penality that traverses all points and supervises every instant in the disciplinary intuitions compares, differentiates, hierarchizes, homogenizes, excludes. In short, it normalizes.").

[264] Scully, *supra* note 92.

educators, so-called "rebellious attorneys,"[265] lawmakers, and community leaders.[266] Just as with teacher training, all grassroots members will require education and training in critical race theory, economics, disciplinary methods, and the specific issues at hand in the particular community.[267]

An educated and unified community is the best solution to injustice. And since exclusionary disciplinary policies affect mostly Black and Latino communities in the United States, concerned Black and Latino parents will need to form a Black and Brown coalition. Such a coalition would require cultural exchanges, educational workshops on Black and Latino histories, and a critical exchange of ideas on how to improve the collective fate of Black and Latino children in public and charter schools.[268] This is a tall order, but such complex issues require complex responses from an informed group.

The grassroots is also the best line of defense against simple lip service from politicians and school administrators.[269] Indeed, grassroots movements have a long and distinguished history in achieving social justice causes in U.S. history.[270] The disproportionate suspensions and expulsions of Black and Latino students in the U.S. and in Massachusetts charter schools

---

[265] The term refers to lawyers who are unsatisfied with the legal and political status quo and who thus want to aid communities in altering unjust laws and policies. *See* GERALD P. LOPEZ, REBELLIOUS LAWYERING: ONE CHICANO'S VISION OF PROGRESSIVE LAW PRACTICE 62-64 (1992).

[266] Scully, *supra* note 92.

[267] *Id.* at 998.

[268] *Id.*

[269] *Id.* at 1005 ("Even when law is enacted, unless citizens monitor the law's utility and effectiveness in achieving its stated goals, the law can easily be rendered insignificant at best, and harmful at worst.").

[270] *Id.* at 1010 (noting that tearing down the school-to-prison pipeline is only the beginning of a larger social justice struggle for the dignity of Black and Latino communities in the U.S.).

is much more than a social justice cause—it is a struggle for the dignity of children of color. I can think of no more important cause than standing with the next generation of Black and Latino youth in the fight to uphold their human dignity in the face of mass suspensions, expulsions, and incarcerations. Indeed, lives and futures are at stake in this battle. Entire communities hang in the balance, especially already vulnerable and marginalized communities of color.

CONCLUSION

*T*he issues in this small book are complex and multifaceted. Thus, the presentation of topics was also parsed strategically. In three parts and multiple subsections, the paper showed how the rise of charter schools and their zero-tolerance polices (reflecting the get-tough stance on crime) has adversely affected Black and Latino students. The schools profiled, coupled with the data, show that Black and Latino students were suspended out-of-school at higher rates than whites for minor offenses during the 2014-2015 school year. The paper also presented some plausible reasons for the discipline gap, including educators' perceptions and policies.

Pursuing judicial solutions to the issue will likely prove unfruitful, since precedent favors giving "reasonable" educators wide discretion in setting and enforcing disciplinary policies. Courts seem unlikely to extend more than minimal protections to students. Educators, policymakers, and the courts justify mass disparate suspensions in the name of school safety and efficiency.

Thus, solutions to the unfair disciplining of Black and Latino students for minor offenses will come from local communities themselves: in the form of legislation, application of restorative practices—instead of punitive practices—in schools, and the emergence of grassroots and concerned citizens who will apply pressure on the legislatures and who will monitor the implementation of any school policies and legislative bills. As Tupac once said: "The power is in the people and politics we address."

In a future book, I will explore more in depth why charter school educators are sweating the small stuff. And how does this relate to law enforcement enforcing minor offenses against Black and Latino males on the street? Is there a plot to overly regulate and discipline Black and Latino communities in the U.S.? If so, this small book is only the start of unraveling that plot—and only a humble beginning in service of grassroots movements who wish to fight for racial justice in the schools and on the streets.

Appendix I
(Chart, broken down by race, of out-of-school suspensions at six Massachusetts charter schools)

School	Racial Group	Disciplined	Out-of-school suspension %
Roxbury Prep	B = 501	B = 209	B = 41.7%
	L = 376	L = 137	L = 35.4%
	W = 10	W = 3	W = 0
	A = 6	A = 0	A = 0
City on a Hill (Dudley)	B = 142	B = 50	B = 35.2%
	L = 48	L = 15	L = 31.3%
	W = 1	W = 0	W = 0
	A = 3	A = 0	A = 0
City on a Hill (New Bedford)	B = 17	B = 6	B = 29.4%
	L = 39	L = 7	L = 15.4%
	W = 30	W = 8	W = 23.3%
	A = 1	A = 0	A = 0
Hampden Charter School	B = 76	B = 9	B = 11.8%
	L = 103	L = 10	L = 9.7%
	W = 162	W = 9	W = 4.9%
	A = 12	A = 0	A = 0
Excel Academy	B = 46	B = 6	B = 13%
	L = 477	L = 35	L = 7.1%
	W = 68	W = 5	W = 0
	A = 13	A = 0	A = 0
Baystate Academy Charter	B = 84	B = 15	B = 17.9%
	L = 151	L = 17	L = 11.3%
	W = 18	W = 1	W = 0
	A = 3	A = 0	A = 0

Appendix II
(Table of Offenses from City on a Hill Charter School Student Handbook)

Level 1 Offenses
3 or more demerits in one class
Derogatory language (Language that may be perceived to violate the civil rights of any person by putting them down because of their gender, race, sexual orientation, religion, culture, ethnicity, national origin or physical or mental disability.)
Not wearing a uniform (Wearing a coat, sweatshirt, or non-CoaH cardigan or wearing boots or sneakers)
Yelling or shouting in class and in the hallway
5 minutes or more late to class without a pass

Level 2 Offenses
Acting inappropriately towards an adult
Horseplay (includes, but limited to, hitting/kicking/wrestling other students, play fighting, and running)
Arguing about demerits
Repeated disruptions of the learning environment
Insubordination (Refusing specific, reasonable instructions (such as saying no, walking away, or repeating an inappropriate behavior) of an adult is insubordination. Some examples of insubordination are: refusing to hand over electronics, refusing to give your name,
refusing to move your seat, refusing to do work in class, or refusing to change inappropriate behavior after repeated redirection.)
Skipping Detention
Repeated Level 1 Offenses

Appendix III
(Federal Sentencing Commission Sentencing Table, 2015)

SENTENCING TABLE
(in months of imprisonment)

Offense Level	Criminal History Category (Criminal History Points)					
	I (0 or 1)	II (2 or 3)	III (4, 5, 6)	IV (7, 8, 9)	V (10, 11, 12)	VI (13 or more)
1	0-6	0-6	0-6	0-6	0-6	0-6
2	0-6	0-6	0-6	0-6	0-6	1-7
3	0-6	0-6	0-6	0-6	2-8	3-9